Brown Girl, Brown Girl, Hasn't Anyone?

A Child's Memoir

by
Michele Jeanmarie

Archway Publishing books may be ordered through booksellers or by contacting:

Archway Publishing
1663 Liberty Drive
Bloomington, IN 47403
www.archwaypublishing.com
844-669-3957

ISBN: 978-1-6657-4882-7 (sc)
ISBN: 978-1-6657-4883-4 (e)

Library of Congress Control Number: 2023915885

Cover illustrated by Aaron Herrera

Print information available on the last page.

Archway Publishing rev. date: 08/17/2023

TABLE OF CONTENTS

CHAPTER 1

GEOGRAPHY

Panama is an isthmus. It is very narrow. It connects North and South America. On one side is the Atlantic Ocean. On the other side is the Pacific Ocean. It can be confusing because some see it as east and west, not Atlantic or Pacific. Some also see it as part of South America, not Central America. This confusion is in part because it is in the shape of an "S," an "S" that is lying down. In school, Chela learned that it is north and south based on the oceans which caress its coastlines.

Because Panama is so narrow, the visionaries of France saw an opportunity for commerce. Ships had to go all around the tip of Tierra del Fuego, when they could simply cut across. A canal will be built to do just that: cut across.

The French did and got broke halfway through the plans! They sold the blueprints to the Americans, who finished it, called it their own, and instituted their own policies. Policies such as segregating nations by their architectural design made it obvious. Policies such as designating areas by race was another. Policies such as assigning the worst land to imported help from the Caribbean islands were still yet another.

Panama was named Panama by the indigenous, because it is teeming with fish. Simply put, the name meant an abundance of fish.

Once known as Silver City, Rainbow City was an American territory, an area in Panama, Central America. It was operated and ran by the Americans. It was on the Atlantic coast. The canal was man's most ingenious creation which made passage from the Atlantic Ocean to the Pacific Ocean possible and in record time.

After the blueprints were handed over, the Americans realized they needed help. Physical labor! They invited Afro-Caribbeans from British owned islands and French owned islands. They worked very hard to find their niches. They could tolerate the heat. They were used to the mosquito. They proved to be invaluable for the building and maintenance of the Canal Zone, the name the entire area would be given.

In time, Panama came to be known as the "Center of the World, Heart of the Universe."

Its center, its heart helped put to sleep Chela many nights. For, Chela had trouble sleeping, always. Daddy took her for many walks along the breakwaters. Breakwaters are boulders, huge rocks placed to break the water and the waves from getting too close to buildings.

On evenings such as these, Chela seized the opportunity to ask lots of questions: where does the breeze start, where does it come from? The wind blows wherever it pleases. What causes the waves? What draws them back? Hm.

This was Chela's lullaby.

CHAPTER *2*

AT HOME

Chela lived in a four-bedroom house. Her house faced the clear blue waters of the Caribbean Sea. The Caribbean Sea is part of the Atlantic Ocean. Her house faces north. No, it faces east. The sun rises in the east, facing her bedroom. So, it is both. That makes it northeast. The breezes that wafted its waves kept them very cool, especially at night.

The area was robust with much flora, flora that interacted with the cool breezes. The foliage of mango trees, avocado trees, coconut trees, and papaya trees swayed to the rhythms of the breezes. The mimosa pudica was a type of grass which closed when touched. It is also known as shame plant, or bashful plant. The Jamaicans called it makah. Chela had a great fascination for them. Hibiscus surrounded her house, along with roses. To the sides and back were the edibles, plants that provided nourishment.

Chela's backyard was lots of fun, for the curious, the adventurous, the wonderer. On downtime, many times, Chela crossed the highway, the Pan-American Highway, for a stroll along the Caribbean Sea. There she found starfish, which she examined, flipped, and returned to the sea.

Further down, there was a gully that played a role in her love for science. She had lots of science homework, from Mrs. Chilcott. Chela once had to note and record the gully's conditions. Another time, she had to observe and record the lifecycle of a tadpole. Other times, she simply sketched what she saw.

In the mornings, upon awakening, Chela was sent to fetch bush leaves from her garden, for tea. In its season, without turning the back porch lights on, Chela used to peek out of the window to watch dozens of crabs scurrying in her backyard. Exploring, like she does! Soon as she turned on the lights, however, they scrambled. They climbed on top of the other, back to safety, through the holes they had burrowed. Back to the sea, they returned. Survival of the fittest!

The holes which they burrowed dried up rather quickly, leaving a basin. These basins created an opportunity for golfing.

At home, in front of her house, the community kids always gathered to play The Rat and the Cat.

Little rat, little rat! What are you doing in my cave?
Looking for something to eat.
With whose permission?
With mine!
Bet I eat you!
Bet you don't
Bet I do!
Bet you don't

Everyone got a chance to run around the circle. First, it was Xiomara, then Roxana, then Carlota, then Carmen, then Yadira, then Yvette, then Suzette, then Amor, then Vielka, and then Maritza. Everyone was tapped to run, but not Chela. She was happy, because at least, her little sister got tapped to run.

Chela was glad it was dusk and time to go in. At 8:00, her favorite commercials would come on and summon her and her little sister to bed!

Let's go to bed
For we need our rest.
So that tomorrow
We can be our best.

The DDT truck was struck to go through the community. The truck sprayed something to keep away the mosquitoes. This spray was poisonous. It would later make people sick…, sick, sick, sick…, very sick. Chela's daddy had heard of other experiments done on people of African descent. Making sure his loved ones were protected from any American experiments, he made sure Mamá knew to call them indoors. That Chela was indoors was most delightful, for there were either biscuits, and milk, and ice cream, and Jell-O.

Dessert!

The following day, after school, the kids of the community gathered again at Chela's house. They chose to play *Matarile*. Two captains were chosen, and each picked their team members. Chela was last to be chosen, but she was happy because Little Sister was first to be chosen.

Again, she had not said anything. She would quickly go in and see her favorite commercial once again. Tomorrow will be another, a better day.

Home was the center point of fun. Chela's eldest brother played in a band. He played the trumpet, the guitar, the electric guitar and the piano. Often, they played on the back porch. When he was not playing music, he was experimenting.

Daddy had gotten him a large piece of plywood, which he called his operating table. On this, he operated on a bat and a frog. He pinned them down, removed their interiors, placed them in some type of liquid in jars, and took them back to school. When a puppy was put down, he brought it home and did the same thing. After cleaning its interior and exterior, he restuffed it and gifted it to Granny. This was his first taxidermy.

Home was also a place for parties. Mamá and Daddy held many dinner parties. The ladies arrived in long gowns. The meals were special, and according to the men in attendance, the drinks from Daddy's bar were also special! Chela's brothers readied the house by trimming the back porch with palm leaves. Both little sisters placed themselves in the middle of the hoopla. Chela could care less. She stayed in her room solving puzzles and figuring out riddles. When it was her big brothers' turn to host their own parties, she did come out on occasion, only to turn on the brightest surrounding lights.

HeeHeeHee!

After their parties was church. Everyone got ready, but Chela's brothers. They wanted to sleep in. Mamá reminded them they are to thank God for their legs to dance.

Chela's brothers were very involved: in after-school activities, that is.

All was not that way, actually. They were very compassionate brothers. In times when Chela had cramps, they cried out for help, on her behalf. Daddy will soothe her belly until Mamá came with the proverbial tea.

A day when Chela was sent to her brothers' bedroom with their folded laundered clothes, Chela caught sight of a magazine.

There was a picture of a beautiful woman on the cover. She knelt down to peruse it, to browse through it. She fanned it first to see if anything would catch her interest. She did not get far, for it opened up to one large picture. She held her head to one side, then another. She flipped the book to one side, then another. Still, Chela could not make out what she was looking at. Daddy peered in and looked over Chela. He gently took the magazine out of her hands. He sent her away to Mamá and called for her brothers. She couldn't decipher much, but what she did, she surmised it had something to do with the magazine. That was not the only time Daddy showed his disappointment.

Chela had taken her dinner juice out to the back porch to finish it. There was a sink on the back porch. She left her dinner juice in the sink, however. Daddy came home and saw the glass of juice. He was angry. He pointed over to the Caribbean Sea, on the other side of the Caribbean Sea, and reminded Chela how much in need the children over there were.

Chela was not wasting the juice. She had simply forgotten it was there.

The matriarch of the family next door had passed. There was a novena for her. There was a funeral, of course. After what was thought to be the end of the mourning period, Chela's brothers put on some American music. Daddy came home from work. He stopped the record player. He reminded them they had to continue mourning for the neighbors.

How long?

CHAPTER 3

POLITICS

Politics around the world was getting messy. There was a conflict between the United States and Cuba. Cuba could no longer export sugar, their primary crop, to Panama. The United States placed an embargo on their sugar. It was difficult to find sugar in all of Panama, except on the Canal Zone. They had no supply shortage. There were no interruptions. They still got sugar. As a resident of the Canal Zone, Chela got sugar, as well.

Bakeries and confectionaries on the Panamanian side were low in sugar. They had no place to which to turn. Daddy did not like that. He purchased a bag of sugar here, a bag of sugar there, and a bag of sugar here and there.

Daddy decided to have a walkabout on one Saturday in the city of Colón, on the Panamanian side. Daddy loaded up the back seat of his Oldsmobile with bags of sugar, upon which he sat Chela and her siblings.

Between the border of Rainbow City and Colón, a checkpoint was placed. A policeman was on guard. He detained the car. Inside, the policeman peered. To the back, the policeman looked. Into his hands, Chela's daddy slipped him a bill. Daddy was let through.

At the confectionary, Daddy unloaded the bags of sugar. The confectioners were delighted. Chela looked on. Chela and little sisters got sweeties.

Chela and her family proceeded on their walkabout. A tall, slender, young man was also on his walkabout. He pranced about, funnily, the length of the park. He found a spot on a bench. He sat funnily. *Maricón.* Chela heard exclaimed. What God has made; no man shall curse. Chela heard Daddy mutter.

CHAPTER 4

AFFINITIES

Chela enjoyed reading a lot. At her school's library, there was an enormous dictionary that sat on the lectern. On the way to her seat, Chela always stopped before it to find any words that stood out to her.

From very young, Daddy recognized Chela's aptitude for the disciplines. He purchased several subscriptions to different types of magazines for her, beginning with Highlights all the way through Seventeen Magazine. He even returned from the States once with a *Roget's Pocket Thesaurus* for her. Another time, he brought back a book on baking.

From this book, Chela chose a caramel cake recipe, which she baked for Daddy. She laid out the ingredients. She followed the recipe.

The batter was beautiful. The batter was tasty. Chela looked away for a moment, and the bowl went out of control. It spun and spun. The batter splattered all over the walls. What a mess! Chela cried. Mamá to the rescue.

Daddy had also brought back an ice cream churner. On the back porch, he gathered Chela and little sister to make ice cream. There was ice all over the ground. There was salt all over, too. It was good, but Chela still preferred the ice cream from the Club House.

The Club House was an establishment set inside the Canal Zone. It was known for the best pastries, the best ice creams, the best hangout, for adults. The teenagers had an after-school club, also, where they went to socialize in a safe supervised environment. Chela never felt comfortable there. Academics were her thing.

At school, Chela was very involved. Chela participated in numerous school activities, even in her community. She wrote articles for the community's newspaper, *The Spillway*, with Mr. Coburn's help, her English teacher. Every day, Mr. Coburn had the class jot down two unknown words from the TV. It was dubbed the American Forces

Radio & Television Service. Chela still remembers the jingle. This station was operated by the armed forces, the GIs, the Ground Infantry, stationed in Panama. In the morning, Mr. Coburn asked for volunteers to share their new words. He proceeded to have them define the words, identify their parts of speech, and use them in sentences, which he then diagrammed. How much fun!

Chela also enjoyed mathematics, and geometry, where lines, segments, triangles, and squares make up dodecahedrons, a favorite word of hers. Mr. Henry was quite the teacher, the maestro, the *profesor*. He was actually a mathematician. He would later influence Chela's methodologies in teaching math.

One day, when he had to step out of the classroom, the students were struggling with the follow-up exercises. One daring student got up, approached *Profe's* desk, looked up the answer in the teacher's edition, and shared it with everyone. Chela had already worked out the problem and warned them the Teacher's Edition answer was incorrect. No one listened. Everyone jot down the answer from the Teacher's Edition. Chela had not. She solved the problem. She was sure of her answer. She did not change her answer.

When grading, *Profe* wondered why so many had gotten the problem right, when Chela had gotten hers wrong. He worked out the problem himself and came up with Chela's answer. What he said next, Chela cannot recall, but he looked at Chela, and Chela looked away.

Busted!

Added to math was her gusto for contemporary art. Chela liked the way it extrapolated her thinking. Chela liked the way art made her think.

She tried her hands in a competition. She painted an abstract drawing, but at the last minute failed to submit it for fear she would fail!

She memorized and rehearsed *The Ant's Picnic* but came in nowhere; well, she became ill!

She presented an oral composition but could not even finish it; well, she started to sob.

She was asked to recite a soliloquy in Spanish but feared she could not fare for fear she could not ferociously roll her r's.

The teacher suggested to Daddy she got her lingual frenulum slightly split. She even recommended a surgeon in Coronado, on the Pacific side, who could perform the surgery. How dare she! No way will Daddy be so presumptuous. If confidence she lacked in rolling her r's, she will find and use synonymous words that did not have many, if at all, any r's.

Chela had given up! Or did she? She would take a chance on the challenges of life. She would continue to make the honor roll, and that was just that.

On the way to her class, Chela saw some scribbling on the exterior wall of her school. She stopped. She read it. She frowned. She thought it was unkind comments about a schoolmate made by another. She leaned down and removed an eraser from her school bag. She erased the comments just when the principal was parking.

Minutes later, she was summoned to his office. She explained. He smiled, thanked her, and sent her back to her classroom.

CHAPTER 5

THE COMMISSARY

Every two weeks, Chela got an allowance. She set aside some for tithing. She kept some for sweeties. The rest she deposited into a bank, where Mamá had helped her to open an account.

At the bank, she was given a bank book. Whenever she went to make a deposit, a teller stamped her book in black ink. The stamps were many. The more stamps she had, the more columns she filled up. That meant her money grew, and in time, enough for a Christmas present for herself. At this time, the teller used, instead, a red stamp to stamp her book. This meant she drew out money, her own money from her account. Her little bank account was something of which she was proud.

Every two weeks, Chela went shopping with her family at the commissary. Shopping was fun. Chela liked seeing how things were designed from the perspective of others. She accompanied Mamá up and down the aisles. They enjoyed perusing the assortment and variety of American provisions. When Mamá finished, the groceries were bagged and taken to the car. The young men liked bagging for mamá. Mamá tipped well. As they were shopping, Chela's daddy had the car serviced. He also tipped well.

The day continued upstairs, in the clothing department, then in the cafeteria, where Chela enjoyed eating American hamburgers and French fries.

Yum, yum.

At Christmas time, Toyland was opened. It was set aside in a warehouse perpendicular to the commissary. During this time, Chela skipped her way to revel in what's hot and new in the world of toys, to see how they were made, to see how they were arranged. On a Panamanian channel, there was a nightly show which featured toys of the season. She often compared what she saw on the American side to what was featured in the Panamanian market.

On the way home, Daddy stopped to visit the Chiney man, an Asian man who made Panama his home. He had a garden. He sold produce from his garden. Although they had just left the commissary, Daddy always stopped at the Chiney man's garden to chit-chat. They sat on a stoop while they chit-chat. Daddy and Mamá enjoyed his bananas and cherries when they became available. They always bought bags of produce from him.

CHAPTER 6

THE CUNAS OF SAN BLAS

On one occasion, Chela recalled shopping in town, on the Panamanian side. Street vendors lined the curbs. One cart stood out, one that caught Chela's eyes. It was owned by the Cunas.

The Cunas are indigenous. They live on San Blas, an island north of Colón. The women dress in beautiful bright-colored cotton tops and bottoms. They wear oversized matching handkerchiefs on the back of their heads, covering much of their hair. Some wear hoop rings through their nostrils. They are married. They maintain their traditions, extending them to their younglings. They don't speak much. They simply nod and respond with bodily gestures when asked about something.

The Cunas are renowned for their arts and crafts, more specifically, their molas. These speak for themselves and, perhaps, the reason why language is not necessary.

Molas are intricate designs. Many of them depict domestic animals, but many can be animals of the rainforest, or even abstract designs. Layers of fabrics are laid on top the other, different sections are cut out, so when they are interfaced, a different color is exposed. To hide the frayed threads, said section is sewn by hand, very tightly, each stroke metered and spaced equidistantly of the other.

At these booths or stands, transactions are negotiated through much haggling and bartering. Daddy frowned upon this and always paid the asking price.

CHAPTER 7

ON THE AMERICAN SIDE

Americans arrived in Panama to make a better living. They held higher positions on the Panama Canal. They did not pay taxes, not to America and not to Panama. In Panama, they used the roads, they used bridges and consumed natural resources.

Although there were lots of African American men in the American Armed Forces, they were not regarded the same as their white counterparts, so when talking about them, they were regarded by their color only.

The Canal Zone was just as segregated as any developed country. Rainbow City housed many of the Afro and French Caribbean people. The houses were great. The roads were great, but per Daddy, theirs were greater.

Chela found that out when she changed schools. She would start at an American school named after Christopher Columbus, *Cristóbal Colón,* in Spanish, Cristobal, in English, no accent mark, for short. So, to be transferred to Cristobal High School was quite eventful for Chela.

At Cristobal High School, Chela would have new friends and new teachers. She knew the teachers would like her, but… others?

Chela was excited. She would get to ride the yellow school bus every morning to go to school. This was free. Before then, at her previous school, her schoolmates of Afro-Caribbean descent had to find their own transportation. They paid for their own transportation. It was public transportation. Because lunch was not provided at school, many had to rush home for lunch.

Chela walked. Chela walked to school in the morning, back home for lunch, back to school for the second half of the day, and back home again. Four times per day! If, for any reason any had to return to school for after-school activity, walking they had to do.

After lunch, dozens had to make the decision to either walk or take a bus back to school. At Cristobal, there was no hustling for the bus. Lunch was provided, although for a fee.

The school was also airconditioned! But much to Chela's surprise, the academics were anything but. After a placement test, Chela was promoted; she skipped to the next grade level. She did not do her tenth year.

Chela missed her Afro-Caribbean teachers. Not one transferred.

It was during Physical Education and Chela's class had been assigned to volleyball. It was a tie game, and Chela's turn to serve. Everyone scurried and got extremely anxious and would not let Chela serve. Xiomara slid past Chela and posted up to serve. But, alas! The teacher turned around and caught her by surprise. She demanded that Chela served.

Chela nervously posted up. She gingerly held the ball in her left hand and swinging her right arm as far back as she could, forcefully struck the ball. Alas! It fell on the opponent's side. Chela's team had scored.

Chela was on top of the hill! She thought about shaping her eyebrows, but Daddy thought her eyebrows were already beautiful. (Years later, if only she had listened, she won't have the need to either fill them in or darken them).

Successive days had gone by, and Chela's friends were not really Chela's friends.

CHAPTER 8

PAN AMERICAN GAMES

At a time when the Pan American Games were held in Panama, Chela and her family drove the distance to see the games. The games were spectacular. They had a wonderful time, but as the Jamaican proverb goes, *chicken merry, hawk is near,* and boy it was!

On the way back, calamity struck! Bump! Bump! Bump! There was a shadow of something that fell on the hood. Each time it bumped, Chela's eyes grew wider. Her shrieks grew even louder. Her bawls more so.

What happened next, Chela could not recall. Who arrived on the scene, Chela could not place. How Chela got home, she could not remember. Who got them home … not even. Chela's mind went blank. That Daddy was on TV, as the French man responsible for the death of a man, who fell off the embankment onto their car, was what Chela recollected. What she did remember was when Daddy kissed her cheek, one late night, upon his release. Was it the same night? Chela's mind is fuzzy.

A French man. Why was it reported like that? Descriptors are necessary, but what does a French man, an Afro-French Panamanian have anything to do with a man losing his balance off an embankment? Years later, Chela had overheard Daddy's friend asking him what has a French man got to do with an Indian woman, her mother.

Chicken merry, hawk is near. The enjoyment they had at the Pan American Games had quickly vanished.

A life was lost. A man was gone. How sad.

CHAPTER 9

OF MERCY AND GRATITUDE

One game day, Chela and her sister were shown to a first-class cabin on a train to an American football game, fifty minutes away, at Balboa High School. Chela's sister did not want to sit in first class. She wanted to be with the others, in the rear. Chela acquiesced and moved to the rear. The conductor nudged them to first class. The conductor knew Daddy. He nudged them back, holding up their tickets, to the front. They nudged back. He dropped his shoulders and consented. In the rear, there was much noise, more rambunctiousness.

Finally, the train halted. Everyone got off, and Chela's sister persuaded her to get off, as well. Chela reminded Little Sister that they were to first visit Daddy's cousin at the hospital. He was an old man. He was much older than Daddy. The hospital was the next stop. Right before the train's whistle, Little Sister jumped off. To keep up with her, Chela jumped, too. Back at home, Chela told. Chela confessed. They had not gone to visit the sick. Disappointment.

Pretty soon, at Cristobal, Chela had gained the students' admiration. She made the honor roll. A roster was posted, and Chela was ranked high.

Soon, Chela began to play tennis, not at Cristobal High School, but on the grounds of her old school, Rainbow City. Little Sister had inspired her to play tennis, so upon getting off the school bus, they got into their play clothes, got their tennis paraphernalia and went to their old school. There, a retired Physical Education teacher, Mr. Loney, coached them. Little Sister soon dropped tennis, but Chela met him diligently and learned from him. She excelled and participated in several tourneys, not ever winning any match. All the same, she felt very comfortable, adding ping pong, then growing in confidence in badminton at Cristobal High.

There, Little Sister took up water polo. This would have made Chela very anxious. She did not like swimming. At her previous school, she made all the excuses in the world to sit out. If only they had not made her get away with that, she would at least, be comfortable in the water.

As time progressed, Chela had grown close to Julie, an American girl, who lived in the Canal Zone most of her life. In the mornings, when Julie got off her school bus, she waited to meet Chela and together they walked to classes.

News had broken that there would no longer be a Rainbow City or a Cristobal High or the Canal Zone. The Canal Zone would become extinct. Julie was very melancholic. As they were walking toward the girls' gymnasium, Julie had said to Chela that she was no longer her friend.

Chela marched on.

CHAPTER 10

CUSTOMS AND TRADITIONS

El 3 de noviembre marked the day that Panama got its independence from Colombia; the year was 1903. Some Colombians remained, for they enjoyed working for the Americans in the Canal Zone. Working for the Americans meant having a reliable income, a home, a hospital, a school for their children, and comfort knowing they'll be safe and secure in their own homes. For when there was a riot, all on the Canal Zone was to remain on the Canal Zone.

Schools on the Panamanian side prepared every year for *el 3 de noviembre*. The occasion called for each school to march in synchronicity and obedience to their respective bands, to the tunes of national anthems and patriotic music. Some had designated twirlers of batons; others had spots for the *polleras* and the *montunos*. These are young women and men who were dressed in national costumes. The *polleras* and the *montunos* danced to choreographed rhythms. Many hotels have their own set of *polleras* and *montunos* to entertain patrons. Even the *bomberos*, or the firefighters, in their starched, crisped uniforms marched. With cornets, and trumpets, and cymbals, and drums and percussions, they marched. They always stole the show, or the parade. They were always last, with good reason!

Neighboring areas were excited to go to this national parade. Chela's community was no exception. In town, the streets were lined with residents both on and off the Canal Zone, visiting relatives, alumni, tourists, and spectators. It was an extraordinary day, as it was every year.

Christmas was soon approaching, most joyous Christmas. Chela loved Christmas. Christmas was made special every year. Although Chela loved to be in school, she too, was jubilant.

The boys were charged with washing the windows and trimming the shrubs around the house. The girls were charged with washing the crystals and trimming the Christmas tree. Daddy always took on the hanging of the Christmas lights, and Mamá took on the baking: a whopping twenty-four fruitcakes. Also known as black cakes, these fruitcakes were very different than those at the commissary.

Back in January, Mamá filled an oversized glass jar with raisins, currants, cherries, prunes, and any dry fruit, which she ground and soaked in Caribbean rum. The recipe arrived when the Afro-Caribbeans were invited to complete the construction of the Panama Canal. Mamá placed this jar on the very top of the cabinet. Periodically, she had Chela or any of her siblings climb to fetch the jar, upon which time, she added more wine, rum, or both.

At Christmastime, Mamá added this macerated jar of fruits to the regular cake batter. She then baked them. She wrapped them individually. She set aside twelve for the New Year's Season. The other twelve cakes were set aside for Christmas guests. They popped in and out without calling first, the norm in Panama. When they called, Mamá served them a slice of fruitcake, a slice of ham, a slice of turkey, and cornichons. Sweet. Bitter. Briny. Peppery. To drink, Daddy offered guests anything from his house bar.

Midnight mass called for rest during the day. Chela was accustomed to this, since throughout the year, they were all required to rest on the Sabbath. After mass, they celebrated Baby Jesus' birth with a glass of Vino Oporto. Then, they got back to bed.

Chela already knew one of the toys she and Little Sister would get. She would get a brown dolly, and Little Sister would get a white dolly. Chela's daddy saw to this. *Brown Girl in the Ring,* a popular song and game, were played by little girls who, one by one, would enter the ring to show off their moves. There was much pride, so how Daddy got hold of a black dolly was not a long stretch. As he worked on the Panama Canal and lived in the Canal Zone, he sent away for one from one of the American department stores. Along with their presents, would be bikes and skates for their cousins, friends of cousins, and orphans.

Besides the dollies, Chela's little sister got a chemistry set. The usual baking soda and vinegar and tube vials, all too common in these sets, satiated her quest for discovery. Following the directions was not enough for her. She thought to double the recipe. She then threw the cotton ball at the TV. Sitting next to the TV was the youngest of them, not much older than a toddler. Fire. The TV caught on fire, so did her face! Rushed to Cristobal Hospital, it turned out to be second degree burns. There is no evidence of scarring ever on her face.

This did not stop there. Little sister inserted a wire into an outlet. What happened next was a blackout. The entire neighborhood had a blackout. All the streetlights were off! Daddy had to call the Maintenance Department!

Sabbaths were celebrated from Fridays at sunset to Saturdays at sunset. Using leftovers from the week, Chela's mother typically prepared soups for supper. Anything else required too much labor. Chela and her sisters played hand games. At noon, they took naps.

At sunset on Saturday, Chela and her sisters had a lot of chores. Chela was sent out to the garden to pick *gandules*. After picking them, she shelled them. She set them aside in a bowl for Sunday's rice.

On Sundays, her chores continued in preparing the coconut. It was quite a laborious task. She cracked the coconut against the concrete of the back porch. She drained the water and reserved it in the refrigerator for any impromptu guests who asked for Coconut Water & Rum. After setting aside the coconut water, she dislodged the meat from the coconut stone, sliced, diced, and blended it. She strained it through a sieve, squeezing out the milk. This milk, in lieu of water, was added to Sunday's rice along with the *gandules*. After desiccating the coconut, she either threw away the coconut flakes or gave them to her neighbor to make *cocaidas*.

One Sunday a month, Chela and her family visited the old people's house. It might be known to some as the convalescent home or the retirement home. Her mother always prepared a huge pot of *"arroz con pollo,"* rice & chicken, the national dish. Most would have this dish on Sundays. While her parents served and visited the old, Chela and Little Sister stormed the mango trees, often scuffing their Sunday shoes. They were never reprimanded for this.

Chela and Little Sister had a set of clothes for everything. School clothes were for school only. Play clothes were for after school. Church clothes were for church. Party clothes, or special occasion clothes were for …well, you get it. They also had handbags and shoes and accessories.

After Christmas came *Carnaval*. Chela liked *Carnaval*. The *Carnaval* was a parade with up tempo rhythms. The town anxiously awaits this time of year. Chela's most joyous part of the *Carnaval* was the end of the parade. It is dedicated to the Soul Queen and her float, which was always spectacular. The Soul Queen is brown. She had to be brown. Every year, she was brown. This year she was also brown. She had to be the prettiest and the most popular of all.

Later, Chela learned she also generated the most money, with fundraisers. She and her family sold the most *frituras: yuca, patacón, carimañola, salchicha and bofe.*

Yum, yum.

This Chela… simply… loved. The *frituras* were good, and to see the reigning beauty was also good. She must be brown, just like her. As her float paraded on, Chela looked on with admiration.

Where there were descendants of Africa, there feared the worship of other gods. To halt this was the goal of Catholicism, for the first commandment calls for one God and one God only. Panama was among the many countries, where slavery and its effects, still stood the risk of this practice. They were permitted to celebrate this revelry of lesser gods during the weeks leading up to Lent, in hopes that with time, they will abandon the practice altogether.

The country joined in through sheer ignorance. Chela's daddy never permitted any icons of lesser gods, masks, and such to cross the threshold of his home. To embrace the culture and show respect, however, he permitted Chela and her siblings to enjoy the festivity at face value only.

The people in the streets danced, beat, and stomped to the rhythms of African beats. Right at sunrise, however, on Ash Wednesday, the country fell into the deep practice of Catholicism. Everyone fasted. Everyone became reverent.

Chela's mamá rode the bus every Friday into town for fresh fish. To eat fish every Friday was a rule to help us to practice obedience. Vatican II, however, abolished it. Daddy continued the practice, nevertheless. The market was particularly crowded on Fridays during Lent. They knew Mamá and her specialties. She never had problems finding her foods.

No one objected to the strictness of the season, because there was Good Friday. Friday was good because sin was overcome. The country fasted yet again. The country dressed in dark clothing on Good Friday. It was a day of mourning. It was a day all Catholic churches processed through town. The people lined the streets to watch the procession, just as they did at *Carnaval* and *3 de noviembre*.

Statues in tow, the parishioners processed down the streets. Solemnly, everyone watched with hope and faith. The faithful pressed on. The spectators were transfixed on the statues. The statues held their gaze, and the faithful kept theirs on them… as though there was dialogue.

Beautiful mystery!

Easter week marked a week of celebration, of rejoicing, for the resurrection of the Lord was near. It was marked with much planning. Mamá baked a few buns, cousins to the hot cross buns, but more pungent, given the Afro-Caribbean spices with which they were made.

On Easter Sunday, Mamá offered impromptu guests a slice of bun, with a slice of cheddar cheese and a slice of ham, and of course, cornichons. They also were invited to Daddy's liquor.

As it was and still is the custom to light candles for special requests and venerations, Mamá honored the practice. Daddy had brought home a candle, too wide for the candle vase holder. Chela could not get the candle in, so she took it to Mamá who was hemming something at the sewing machine. Mamá could not get the candle into the vase, either. She had Chela hold the vase, as she tried to shimmy it. Trying one more time, a bit more forcefully, Mamá pushed it down breaking the candle the vase. The vase cut Chela's thumb from one side of her thumb nail to the other side of the thumb nail. Mamá called for help. Her brother, practicing with his band on the back porch, barged into the hysteria. Bawling, someone held down Chela, while someone else poured salt into the wound.

The funny thing is, there was no blood. At least none that Chela could remember. Was she taken to the doctor? Did she get any stitches? No memories, but only a thick scar that has shrunk with age and evidence she had not gotten any stitches, and that there must have been blood, lots of it.

Chela's family had a knack for taking the natural approach. Chela was fearful of heights. On a trip to Panama City, Daddy thought he would knock out that fear. He stopped in the middle of a bridge. Chela cried and cried and cried. It took another car to get him going.

CHAPTER 11

THE PANAMA CANAL TREATY

Chela's family decided to leave for the United States, after Lent. President Jimmy Carter and Omar Torrijos were successful in getting the Panama Canal Treaty ratified. It was a document that gave all residents of the Canal Zone the choice to move and settle in any part of the United States. It also returned the Panama Canal back to the Panamanians. It involved training local Panamanians in the intricacies of the Panama Canal, its governing body and the infrastructure of the Canal Zone. As the Panamanians became adroit in handling each section, that sector would return to the Panamanian people and its government. As others were leaving and settling in the States, those who wanted their homes and positions slid into those spaces. Unfortunately, Omar Torrijos was assassinated. No one was ever able to find the killer.

President Jimmy Carter will forever be the servant leader. He raised the standard of living of the entire country. He always thought of others, taking the least popular position, ahead of his own ego. Of great character and compassion, the Panama Canal Treaty, and eventually, Habitat for Humanity would become his legacy.

Yes, President Jimmy Carter will forever be a servant leader, and Omar Torrijos will forever be remembered as the one for the people, *el pueblo.*

Chela and her sisters had to organize all which they were to take to the United States. The items they could not pack, or no longer wanted, were taken to the orphanage.

Daddy chose California as their new adopted home. California's weather was like Panama's. Because Panama sits low, it was not in the path of hurricanes. It was this that made Panama even more conducive to the operations of the canal and invulnerable to atmospheric destruction. California was known for its earthquakes, but this did not deter Daddy.

Upon landing in California, in Customs, Chela's family was split up. Each was taken to a different room, with a different person. Chela was asked a series of questions, one of which was what she had for breakfast.

"Tea."

"What kind of tea?"

"From the garden."

Later, she learned they were all asked the same questions to verify they were who they said they were. They settled into their new home in California.

CHAPTER 12

THE STATES

The States! Chela was deliriously happy. She would have new friends and new teachers. She knew the teachers would like her, but will her friends?

Chela grew up knowing she was brown. Even at Cristobal High School, she was seen as brown. In the States, however, she was seen as black, until she spoke Spanish.

"What are you?" was a question she often was asked, as though they had never seen a black or brown person who spoke Spanish. This included the Latinos, or was it the Hispanics, or was it the Chicanos? Knowledge of history and the lack of it was very apparent from the bat.

Chela learned that distinctions were made to limit one's upward ascension on the social ladder. After all, it

was Sarai,
from the book of Genesis,
the very first book of the Bible,
from way back then,
who refused to have her son, Isaac,
partake in the inheritance with his Egyptian slave half-brother.
Was it really Sarai who started that distinction?

Chela learned that men used the Bible to justify their own abuses of other men. Had they sought to explore further on, they would have found that they had to release their slaves after the seventh year in bondage! It is well known that developed countries kept their slaves beyond that.

Chela would omit to answer any questions pertaining to race.

Life in the United States for Chela was quite the feat.

She missed Miss Anita. Miss Anita came in every Wednesday to iron their clothes. Now, Chela had to iron her own clothes. They all did.

Mamá learned to drive. She got a job outside of the house. Things were not as rosy and peachy as they were in the Canal Zone.

But Chela was glad the people of Panama got what was rightfully theirs. She was glad several thousand were elevated. Chela was happy for them, although she was not quite as comfortable as she was in the Canal Zone. Julie knew this. No wonder she did not want to be friends, anymore.

Daddy decided to send Chela and her sisters to a school in a Jewish neighborhood. He knew this would be closest to the education and faith with which he raised them.

At school, Chela got good grades. The classes, she found, were easy. The teachers, she found, were amicable. The students she found treated her with indifference.

Whenever Chela spoke in English, she spoke with a heavy accent. She was asked to repeat the same thing several times. Chela was ashamed of the way she spoke. So, she sought out new friends, friends who could speak Spanish. Chela was put in an advanced Spanish class. Soon, she was answering all the questions, made straight A's, and helping the teacher translate documents. Chela's Spanish speaker friends were not really her friends.

What is a friend, anyway?

King David had a great one in Jonathan. Not everyone is promised the same gifts. Such a gift was not to be Chela's. She was given other gifts.

But who was this brown girl, anyway?

Brown girl who was raised in Rainbow City, Canal Zone,
An occupied area in Panama that belonged to the United States of America,
Where segregation still loomed,
Went to an American school led by Afro-Caribbean-educated teachers,
Who was later transferred to an American school in Cristobal,
Who spoke English as her first language,

But spoke Spanish as early as she can remember, because she was
born and raised in a Spanish-speaking country,
Confused about who really were her friends,
Further confused about race and ethnicity,
child of an Afro-Hindu mother who was born in Costa Rica, and
an Afro-French father, who was first generation Panamanian, and
whose first language was French patois.
Brown girl, brown girl, hasn't anyone?

Printed in the United States
by Baker & Taylor Publisher Services